BERKSHIRE PRIVIES

Uniform with this volume

COTSWOLD PRIVIES

by Mollie Harris

CUMBRIAN PRIVIES

by John Dawson

EAST ANGLIAN PRIVIES

by Jean Turner

HAMPSHIRE PRIVIES

by Ian Fox

KENT PRIVIES

by Dulcie Lewis

NORTHAMPTONSHIRE PRIVIES

by Julie Wilson

YORKSHIRE PRIVIES

by Len Markham

BERKSHIRE PRIVIES

by

IAN McLOUGHLIN

COUNTRYSIDE BOOKS

NEWBURY · BERKSHIRE

First published 1997
© Ian McLoughlin 1997

COUNTRYSIDE BOOKS
3 Catherine Road
Newbury, Berkshire

ISBN 1 85306 450 5

Produced through MRM Associates Ltd., Reading
Printed by Woolnough Bookbinding Ltd., Irthlingborough
Typeset by Techniset Typesetters, Newton-le-Willows, Merseyside

CONTENTS

FOREWORD

The county of Berkshire is a little world where state of the art technology rubs shoulders with rural idyll. In the east of the county, there are scientists working on space travel. In the west, there are farmers who spend sleepless nights in barns with pregnant ewes at the start of the lambing season – as their ancestors did centuries ago.

I think you will find that these pages reflect that difference, and it is true to say that there are far more old privies still standing in gardens in the western half of the county than in the east. During my long research, lots of people were kind enough to share their memories with me, and I have set them out as faithfully as I can.

This book is dedicated to its many contributors, who either told me their marvellous stories, or did not shy away from the wild-eyed lunatic confronting them on their doorsteps, asking to photograph the deepest recesses of their old toilets.

My special thanks go to Councillor David Liddiard, a retired farmer in West Berkshire, for all his help. He shall be known henceforth as 'The Privy Counsellor'.

IAN McLOUGHLIN

[1]

IN DAYS OF OLD

There are still old privies around in the most surprising places. This pair of back-to-backs is behind a row of houses on the A4 at Chapel Street, Thatcham, one of the busiest roads in the west of the county. Both have long relinquished their former duties, and are now used as storage sheds.

Our ancestors were a mucky lot. They would have been completely bemused at today's toilet habits, with soft paper and scented soap. For them, nature's functions could be performed almost anywhere, and if someone was watching, so what?

Even when they got the hang of using the little shed at the bottom of the garden, they would still tip the contents of their privy buckets all over the vegetables. And the gardens bloomed wonderfully well. They saw it as a sort of natural recycling, giving back to the earth what they had taken from it. Much better than sending all the stuff down a pipe to a sewage works, so they can filter it and sell it back to you as drinking water. I suppose ecology depends upon your point of view.

When the Romans came here 2,000 years ago, they brought with them their notions of fastidious cleanliness, including the forerunner of the flush loo. Roman engineers built surprisingly modern structures to house baths and lavatories – a word which itself is derived from the Latin *lavabrum*, a bath. They knew how to make lead pipes through which they could send water anywhere they wanted, as long as it was downhill. These were used to pipe water into the loo and flush away the ordure, usually into the river. Because there weren't so many people about, it didn't cause much of a pollution problem.

When the Roman regime collapsed in about AD 400, all this changed. The civilised Romano-Britons were driven out and fled to Brittany or Wales. They were replaced by hordes of Saxon invaders who conquered the land and then settled down to farm it, in a very rough and ready way – which included recycling their natural fertiliser, wherever they happened to be.

The Saxons were not city people, and they did not take up residence in the abandoned Roman farms and villas, of which there were many. It seems strange that they should shun the beautiful stone houses that were up for grabs. All they had to do to make them habitable was to bury the bodies of the previous

Built on steep ground in the back garden of a cottage at Winterbourne, this old wooden privy is now leaning at a rather alarming angle. In times gone by, there was a pigsty next door to it, and the manure from both buildings was spread on the garden, which is absolutely blooming.

11

inhabitants. But the Saxons were used to living in draughty wooden sheds in their native Schleswig-Holstein, and they set about cutting down trees and putting up barns. They ignored the elegant villas – except to occasionally use them as quarries. Their sanitary arrangements were as primitive as everything else about them. If they felt the call of nature, they went behind a bush. Some probably didn't even bother with the bush.

This was a tradition to be stoutly defended by Englishmen for hundreds of years, and can still be seen regularly in many parts of the less developed world.

The phenomenon of the garden privy is comparatively recent in history, as the population grew and notions of cleanliness and propriety entered the confused minds of our forebears. But the old way of nipping behind a hedge carried on in tandem, even into living memory, which goes some way towards explaining why so many of our country lanes and bits of unused ground are abundant with nettles and dock leaves. The plants flourished on this healthy fertiliser, conveniently delivered by the local populace on their way to work in the fields. In his famous book *Cider with Rosie*, author Laurie Lee refers to his elderly female neighbours sneaking off into the woods, rather than use the bucket in the privy, which they would have to empty as soon as it was filled up.

Although the rough and ready Saxons weren't in the slightest bit bothered about hygiene, there was a small remnant of the island population who were. Christianity came to Britain in Roman times, and the monks' institutionalised lifestyle reflected their roots in that civilisation. They were an industrious lot, and built abbeys and monasteries which were – some still are – architectural wonders, considering the only power they had was their own strength and that of their animals, harnessed to ropes and pulleys. Far from putting them off, the hard work of moulding the landscape to suit themselves seems to have driven the monks to extraordinary lengths to build their monasteries to perfection.

Their sanitary arrangements were no different. The monks lived in quite close confinement, with large numbers of them cheek by jowl, eating and sleeping together. This meant if one man caught something nasty, the chances were that they all did. Common sense meant they had to be hygienic. The Saxon peasants, out in the countryside, did not suffer the same problems of being squashed up together, and they would move around to find new grazing for their livestock. So the monks built baths and toilet facilities into their great houses, modelled on a somewhat simpler version of the Roman system.

Very little remains of the architecture of the Saxon period, and it was several hundred years later that there was a boom of monastery building under the new Norman kings, many of whom were just as barbaric in their personal habits as the Saxons before them.

Reading Abbey was founded in 1121 by Henry I, who probably reckoned it a good move to ensure an untroubled passage through the afterlife. It was built on land between the Thames and the Kennet rivers on the eastern side of the town, and some of the remains of it can still be seen today. The abbey flourished and became one of the wealthiest in the country, until Henry VIII threw out all the monks in 1539. Ten years later the buildings were in ruins.

But enough remains, even to this day, to see how the monks' sanitation system worked. It was simple, but very effective. The monks called their loo the 'necessarium', and it consisted of planks with holes cut in them, flushed from below by running water. A part of the Kennet river was diverted in order to achieve this. The stream known as 'Holy Brook' went under one end of the toilet block and out the other, back into the main part of the river. Such a thing would never be allowed in modern times, but one has to remember that the population then was a fraction of what it is now, and that the monks did filter the outgoing water to use the ready supply of fertiliser on their vegetable patch. Their system certainly worked, and indeed saved many of them from the ravages of the Black Death in the 14th century, when half the population of England was wiped out by the plague, borne by rats which had been in contact with the filth of primitive city sewers.

Apart from the monks, no one paid much heed to the means of dealing with the call of nature. Before the abbey was built, many of the new Norman feudal lords were busy building castles from which they could bludgeon the people of the countryside into submission. Wherever they could, the Normans would build a moat round the castle, which often served as a ready made drain for its inhabitants' waste products. The fact that most of the moats were stagnant and reeked disgustingly was perhaps beyond the limited sensitivities of these robust people. They also incorporated 'garderobes' into the outer walls of their castles. These little rooms served the dual purpose of being used to store clothes, and as a primitive privy whose products oozed down a pipe to plop into the moat below.

City sanitation was the worst, however. At one time, there were over 100 houses on London Bridge, with only one privy. Not surprising that the inhabitants emptied their pots into the river below – to the annoyance of the sailors. No wonder they took to wearing sou'westers.

These jerry pots, or 'gesunders' were not unfamiliar to the more prosperous people of medieval times either and were originally made of pewter. In 1418 the first earthenware ones appeared, and in later years it became fashionable to decorate them, often with a large eye painted inside on the bottom. During the Napoleonic Wars, Napoleon Bonaparte's face adorned the inside of many a good potty. Adolf Hitler suffered the same fate in more recent times. Poets got in on the act too, with one of the most popular potty inscriptions being: 'Use me

Crapper opened opulent showrooms in King's Road, Chelsea.

EARTH CLOSET TANKS ON WHEELS.

No. 1	1ft. 6in. × 1ft. 1in. × 1ft. 6in. high	£1 6 0
No. 2	2ft. × 1ft. 6in. × 1ft. 9in. ,, ...	1 8 0
No. 3	2ft. 6in. × 1ft. 4in. × 1ft. 9in. ,, ...	1 10 0

If without Wheels—

No. 1	... ...	£1 1 0
No. 2	... ...	1 2 6
No. 3	... ...	1 5 0

"YEARSLEY'S" PATENT GULLEY CLEANER.

A price list from the catalogue of A. Bell & Co. Ltd.

well and keep me clean, and I'll not tell what I have seen.'

It was the institutional privy that caused the worst problems, in terms of both comfort and hygiene. Failure to follow in the footsteps of the monks resulted in huge pits being dug to dispose of the muck created by large numbers of people crammed in together. The pits quickly filled up, and had to be emptied. Digging out the pit and carting away its contents was a job no one wanted to do. But where there's muck there's brass, so they say, and market forces meant that the men who performed this stomach-churning task earned wages which would make even the directors of today's privatised industries green with envy. At Newgate Gaol in 1281 it is recorded that a team of 13 men known as 'gongfermors', or professional cesspit cleaners, took five nights to clear the 'cloaca', at a cost of four pounds seven shillings and eightpence – three times the normal rate, and a lot of dosh in those days.

The first fledgling flush loo made its appearance during the reign of Queen Elizabeth I. Her godson, Sir John Harington, invented a contraption which was installed at Richmond Palace. Her Majesty didn't seem too impressed, and the world continued to do its business largely out of doors for the next couple of hundred years.

By the end of the 18th century, when mad King George III was on the throne, a cabinet maker by the name of Joseph Bramah was making water closets for the gentry. The standard of his products was so high that his name remains today as an indication that something is of the best quality.

Another man whose name lingers with us is Mr Thomas Crapper, who set up in business in Chelsea in the 1870s to mass produce the water closets which have become so much part of our lives. He was the man who refined the cistern which delivers a set amount of water into the bowl at the pull of a chain or turn of a handle. The only noteworthy improvement has been the 'blue bag', of the 1990s, intended to save even more water.

But WCs were a long time coming to the remoter – and in lots of cases the not so remote – parts of Berkshire. Read on for some earthier memories that are still vivid for many people in the county.

[2]

'It Was A Long Walk At Night'

Little Park Farm at Mortimer has been farmed by the Froom family for generations and is part of the Englefield Estate. It is quite likely that the privy, well remembered by Miss Pamela Froom from the days before the plumbing was installed, is not that much younger than the house itself, which was built in 1712. Once a magnificent three-holer, it is now in a dilapidated state, and has begun to lean rather drunkenly over the dried out stream bed into which its contents used to be discharged. It was a dog kennel for some years but is now deserted except for the pair of robins that have built a nest in the rafters.

'It was a long walk at night,' recalls Miss Froom.

One of the barns at the farm was built and used exclusively to house farm vehicles. Carts, carriages and horse ploughs were stored inside, and one long dead but considerate forebear had a pit dug in the corner and installed a small privy for the benefit of the farmhands.

GONE TO EARTH

In 1860 a Dorset clergyman by the name of Rev Henry Moule developed what became known as Moule's Earth Closet. While all around him were feverishly tinkering with early models of the flush loo, Rev Moule really went back to basics, cleanliness being next to godliness, and all that.

His invention was ecologically sound, and did not waste gallons of water like we do today, although it was considered unsporting for a gentleman to use one when he did not need to sit down.

DRAINAGE OVER DITCH AT LITTLE PARK PRIVY, THE MAIN HOUSE WAS BUILT IN 1712.

FAMILY SEATING WAS USUAL BECAUSE OF LONG WALK FROM HOUSE AT NIGHT

Drawing kindly supplied by Miss Pamela Froom of Mortimer.

It consisted of an ordinary privy with a seat and a bucket underneath. At the back and above the seat was a hopper containing ashes or fine, dry soil. When a handle was pulled, a measured quantity of ash or soil fell down a chute and covered the contents of the bucket, which was emptied as often as necessary. If you remembered to empty the bucket, and fill up the hopper, it worked fine. The resulting mixture quickly became sterile and hardly ponged at all, which meant it was more easily disposed of.

A high-tech variant of Moule's system was tried and quickly disposed of. An automatic version which set the ash in motion down the chute was triggered by the user rising from the seat. Unfamiliar with the noise of the machinery, startled people would rush out of the privy, pulling up their trousers as they went, convinced it was about to explode.

Moule's idea never really caught on, and as far as I am aware, there are none left in the county. Miss Pamela Froom tells me there was a pair of them at Mortimer Hill, a fine old house on the edge of the village. The mechanism has now been removed, and the building is completely obscured by a huge yew tree.

Miss Froom remembers, 'It was built at the side of the house for the use of people out hunting or shooting. When they got back from the hunt, rather than rush into the house in their muddy boots, they could use the earth closet in the yard.'

Good sound sense, but redundant with the advent of the Portaloo.

Mrs Josie Healey of Cippenham has a friend, Mrs Joan Webb, aged 86, who lived as a child in the village. For her, the privy was a plank with a hole in it, a bucket underneath, in a small hut, a very long way down the garden.

When her father put the cottage up for sale, a young couple came to view it. They fell in love with the place, it was just

The old privy at Little Park Farm, Mortimer, now barely visible behind the foliage that has grown up around it.

what they wanted. The only drawback was that the lady was not happy about the privy being so far away from the cottage.

Joan's father thought they were worried about thieves getting into the privy. He said, 'I can't see why you are so worried about it. We have lived here for 50 years, and we ain't lost a bucketful yet.'

NASTY NETTLES

Mrs Evelyn Alsbury of Beechfield, Frilsham, was aged 88 when she wrote to me. She said: 'I well remember the old privy. When I was a child, we had one at the top of the garden. It was a little brick hut with a seat inside with two holes, one for adults, one smaller for children. There was a trench we sat over, and this had to be cleaned out once in a while.

'When I was six years old, we moved and had a little shed with a seat and a bucket. A hole was dug in the garden in which to empty the bucket.

'At school, it was a brick building with six toilets, three for girls, three for boys. There was a wall between us. Here again it was seats with buckets, and hinged flaps at the back for empty-ing. The boys would wait until we girls were seated, and would then open the flaps, and up would come the nettles, stinging our bottoms.

'It was always a seat and bucket in an outside shed until I married, even here, our cottage had a brick privy at the bottom of the garden. This seat had three holes, father, mother and chil-dren. Here again we sat over a trench, and there was a bucket of ashes and we had to put on a shovelful after use. I cut up news-papers into squares and put a string through one corner to hang it up by. On winter nights we had a candle lantern to light our way. I would not like it now that I am 88 years old.'

This privy for farmhands at Little Park Farm has now sadly deteriorated and is no longer in use – but you can just see the long shovel they used to dig it out.

Mrs Dorothy Austin lives in Newbury, but was brought up on a farm where the privy was next to the pigsty, quite a common location in Berkshire. Here is her story.

'When I was six or seven years old, my sister and I – she is 15 months younger than me – went to the outside loo together. While we were there, my brother, who is two years older than me, and who always rode to the loo on his bike, wanted to use the loo as well, but we girls wouldn't let him in.

'On the grass outside was a tray of very rotten apples, brown and squashy. My brother tried to remove us from the loo by throwing these rotten apples through the air gap at the top of the door. Unfortunately, the apples stuck all over the newly whitewashed wall.

'My brother got fed up of waiting and wandered off, so we were able to come out and go back to the house.

Moule's Earth Closet, 1860.

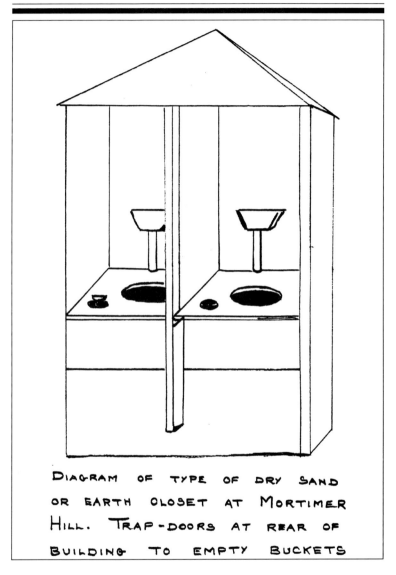

DIAGRAM OF TYPE OF DRY SAND OR EARTH CLOSET AT MORTIMER HILL. TRAP-DOORS AT REAR OF BUILDING TO EMPTY BUCKETS

Miss Pamela Froom's drawing of the Moule's earth closet at Mortimer.

'A few minutes later, my mother went out to use the loo, and immediately saw this brown squashy stuff all over the walls. She thought we had been playing with what was down the holes. Was she angry! She came shrieking back to the house to smack us, but calmed down a bit when we told her it was rotten apples. We always used torn up newspaper in the loo, torn into squares and threaded onto string and hung on a nail. It had a wooden bench seat with two holes in it, and was emptied at the back. This was covered with a piece of corrugated tin and often the loo would not be emptied until the paper tickled your bum. There were several men working on the farm, and they came round with a horse and a small cart and shovelled the toilet out.'

UNEXPECTED GUESTS

Mr L. T. Cooke lived in Russell Road, Newbury, at the only house with an outside privy which contained a flush loo.

'I am 81 years of age and was born in Newbury. We had a loo at the bottom of the garden and I believe it was the only one in the road with a flush toilet. The water cistern was high up and was covered each winter with an old blanket to keep it from freezing up.

'It had a large wooden seat, and I used to have to go with my sister in the dark nights to light the candle. On one such night, she went in, only to run out, screaming. I had to go in, and what had upset her was two huge toads sitting on the seat. The loo was a favourite place for them.'

Mr Cooke's father, Thomas Cooke, was the last of the lamp-lighters in the town. 'It was his job to light the gas lamps in the streets each evening, and then put them out every morning.'

A fine example of a two-holer, now on view at the Chiltern Open Air Museum, Chalfont St Giles.

DOWN THE HOLE

Mrs Diana Garland's father was a herdsman who came with his family to live at Brightwalton. She was eight years old, and considered the privy at the cottage to be the height of luxury. 'It was attached to the house, just a short walk away – not the usual trek to the bottom of the garden, often past the neighbours.

'This toilet had twin seats, one large and one small, both with lids. There was an open pit, which my father daily spread with straw and Jeyes disinfectant. I can't remember the method of disposal, but I think it was emptied rather like the septic tanks of today.

'One evening we were all indoors when my two year old sister needed to go. My father asked me to take her, and I was very cross as I was reading *Black Beauty* at the time.

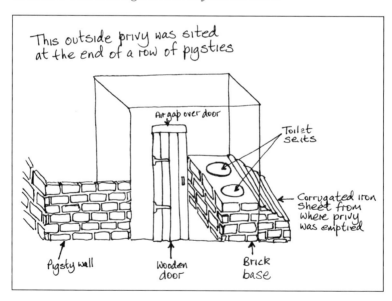

Mrs Austin's privy.

'I flounced off, dragging her along with me. When we were in the lav, she kicked up a fuss because she wanted to sit on the big seat – even I didn't sit on the big one.

'Well, I plonked her on it, and I think you can guess what happened – she went straight through. I rushed panic stricken to fetch my father, and he grabbed a pitchfork and managed to hook her dress and pull her out. We thanked God – my father had just laid fresh straw.

'I have never forgotten the one and only smacking from my father, and I never did finish reading *Black Beauty*. I am now in my sixties, and alas neither my father nor my sister are still here.'

A GOOD READ

Long before the days of soft pink paper on a roll, newspapers would be torn up into squares and a string threaded through one corner, then hung on a convenient nail. But you were lucky if you could get the bit with the end of the story on it, although searching for it was all part of the fun. Favourite papers included the *News of the World*, *Old Moore's Almanack* – and Gamages catalogue.

During the last war editions featuring portraits of Hitler were particularly popular.

Mrs Sandra White now lives in Reading, but grew up in a cottage in the country between Tilehurst and Calcot in the 1940s and 50s.

'I was born in 1946 and lived in a 500-year-old beamed cottage with a home-built privy about 60 feet from the back door. It was a very sturdy and roomy construction, made by my father,

This old copy of the *Daily Mail* commemorates the events of D-Day, 1944.

This charming and unusual row of thatched cottages on the river Kennet at Leverton, near Hungerford, had the privies built in between the houses. How convenient.

approximately four feet wide by three feet deep and seven feet high – my father was six feet two inches tall – made from overlapped wooden planking that was creosoted every year. It was partly hidden by a nut tree.

'The door let in the light through gaps at the top and bottom, which also helped to ventilate the place. My father made the box seat over the pit below, no fancy toilet seats for us, just a well sanded hole cut out of the box. As a child, I used to be fascinated by the numerous postcards, some funny, some pictorial, which were pinned to the walls and would spend my time trying to work out why the adults found the seaside ones so funny.

'If I needed the privy in the dark, mum would light the Tilley lamp and take me there and stand guard outside. As I grew older, about eight, I was able to make the journey by myself

Uncle Ted's old privy at Beedon Hill — See page 34.

with the aid of a torch.

'When visitors arrived, my mother would hurriedly drench the pit with Jeyes Fluid, then cover it with newspaper that she saved for such occasions, to make anyone's visit to the privy slightly more tolerable.

'I should add that around the edge of the cesspit grew the most beautiful rhubarb.

'At the age of 13, we moved from our old cottage to a new house down the road that had an indoor flush toilet and a beautiful warm mahogany seat – what bliss. But I still have fond memories of my very happy childhood in our cottage with the outside privy.'

Uncle Ted's remote privy — See page 34.

GREAT UNCLE TED

Mr Victor Pocock, a retired schoolteacher and keen historian, tells of an extra-long walk to the privy:

'My great uncle, Edward Townsend, lived at Beedon Hill with quite a large family. He had to cross the old A34 Preston to Winchester trunk road before he could get to his toilet, which was about 50 metres away on the other side of the road from the house. The small brick building was demolished when Churches Gate was built some years ago.

'It was extremely difficult to cross the road during the last war, especially around D-Day in 1944. Later, when Uncle Ted was over 80 and nearly blind, the lorry drivers used to stop and help him across. The traffic increased dramatically after the war, and in 1977 it was so great that the present bypass was built. After he died and my great aunt and her daughter moved from the house, an Elsan chemical toilet was installed in the old woodshed. Later still, a flush toilet replaced it.'

[3]

BUCKETS AND A BOMB

Don Lindsay of Newbury remembers the days of privies very clearly. 'I was born in the sticks, to the north of Newbury,' he told me and went on to recall his experience of the pit and the bucket.

'The buckets I know of held about four or five gallons I should think, and it was disposed of by father digging a hole in a fallow piece of the vegetable garden and dumping it. Care had to be taken to remember where the last lot went. One old fellow I know just poured it between the rows of green stuff. After a day or two, when it had dried out a bit, the wind would get hold of bits of the *News of the World* or *John Bull* and plaster them against the neighbour's hedge, which made it very colourful.

'Our dunnikin, or dyke, as Dad called it, backed onto next door's, and I remember the kids in there banging their heels on the board at the front of the bucket, singing "I'm on the lav". This lasted until about 1935, when we moved to a council house, still with no flush loo, until Mother decided the bucket had gone on long enough, and bought an Elsan. It still had to be emptied, and I recall the strong smell of Jeyes Fluid.

'My grandfather was still using the earth closet, which was spread with ashes at intervals. It was dug out regularly and went onto the vegetable patch. Nothing was wasted.

'Our dyke was about 20 yards from the back door, and was not very pleasant on a belting wet night in February. At night time, we all had a "gesunder", which was not to be over-filled. Up to the first joint of the thumb was the limit. This went out under the back hedge, along with all the other household slops. Some old dears who lived nearby used to take it across the high road and chuck it under the farmer's hedge. Nothing much grew in those places.

'All these goings on produced plenty of flies, which reminds me of the townie who came to visit his old Gran. He wanted to use the John, but was driven back by the flies. He complained bitterly to Granny, who told him "Well, if thee can hang on a bit, I'll be getting dinner, and then they'll be all up yere in the kitchen. Then thee can go."

'Most of the country pubs had the loos outside, open to the stars, and with a smell that would knock you over. But we didn't seem to come to much harm, for all that.

'I recall going to London in my uncle's Triumph car one day in the early 1930s. As we went past what is now Heathrow Airport, I noticed a field covered in paper. Uncle told me it was "night soil" brought out from London and spread on the market gardens.

'All the animal excreta was spread on the land, so why not the human, like they still do in the East.

'I must say, I prefer the present system, apart from the terrible waste of water, and I suppose it would be impossible for the population to carry on the old way. Nevertheless, previous generations seemed to manage, although probably not quite so well in the towns.

'When we were out playing, if we got took short, we would go into the nearest hedgerow. A large dock leaf, doubled over, was the favourite. It was cool and clean, the only trouble was, your finger often popped through.

'The buckets were substantially made, with a hefty carrying handle and a handle at the back for ease of emptying. They were oval shaped, and many of them ended their lives dumped in the disused chalk pits where all the rest of the junk went. There were old 9 volt radio batteries, Camp coffee bottles, four-pound treacle tins and pop bottles with a marble in the top.

A farmyard privy that has been carefully restored and is on show at the Chilterns Open Air Museum at Chalfont St Giles. The museum has saved a large number of historic small outbuildings that would otherwise have been destroyed. It has a chapel, a village meeting room, and even a reconstruction of an Iron Age village.

'When I was a lad, one of my jobs was to tear up six-inch squares of the *Newbury Weekly News*, *News Chronicle*, *Daily Herald* or *News of the World*. The squares were hung on a nail on the loo door, and one could sit and meditate on the state of the world, read last week's fatstock prices, or Baldwin's speeches.

'Happy Days!'

Victor Pocock, whose great uncle Ted's snug but oddly located privy is described in the previous chapter, now lives at Beedon. He has vivid recollections of life before the flush, including being in the privy when bombs fell on Newbury in 1943.

'When I was a young boy, it was rare for me to be able to use a flush toilet, as most of them were only in towns such as Newbury. I remember that while visiting relations in Hounslow it was quite a novelty for me to use a water closet or have a bath with hot and cold running water from the tap.

'The lavatory, as it was usually called, at the council houses in Graces Lane, Chieveley, was like a small outdoor shed with a green door built at the back of the house. On one occasion, before we moved to Beedon, I heard, whilst sitting on the lavatory, what seemed to be several bumps some way away. I hurried outside and saw the aftermath of the bombs that fell on Newbury on 10 February 1943. They damaged the council school, St John's church and some almshouses. I could see the dust rising from the effect of the bombs.

'Some years before this, when we lived at Downend, my father constructed a wooden toilet at the top of the garden. One stormy night it blew over, but fortunately nobody was in it at the time.

'The lavatories at Chieveley school and Beedon school were always places to avoid in those days, because of the unhygienic conditions, especially when the buckets needed emptying. A letter from Berkshire Education Committee to Beedon school in

The privy cum washhouse at Purton Stores, Beedon.

1913 says "Your managers have appointed John Smith (my grandfather, the water carrier) as Offices Man." This meant he was given the job of emptying the buckets.

'When we moved to Beedon in 1944, to the shop at Purton Stores, the toilet was about 30 metres away from the house and was in use until the 1960s. It was a brick and tiled structure, hidden behind a hedge. It had a chocolate coloured door, which was the usual colour for Lockinge Estate cottages at this time, but it had no windows.

'As well as a toilet paper holder, there was usually a calendar hanging on a nail. The door always had to be kept open except when it was dark, when a torch was used for lighting. I remember creeping up the path, heart pounding, the trapdoor of my pyjamas hanging up by one button.

Interior of the Purton Stores privy.

'I suppose the worst time was when it rained, and you just had to make a dash for it. You were always afraid your candle would blow out.

'I remember the problems we had during the freeze-up in 1947, when we had to go through snowdrifts in the dark to reach the toilet. But, in an emergency, chamber pots could be used indoors. Before we grew up, Mum or Dad had to come with us, as we were afraid of the dark. During the daytime, the door had to be kept partly open, and one day a young girl from Ashridge Farm came across the fields into the garden and saw me sitting on the dyke, as we called it. I found the situation most embarrassing next day when the young lady told the other pupils on the school bus what she had seen.'

[4]

COUNTRY LIFE

Miss Evelyn Taylor was 93 when she died in February 1997. She spent the last of her days at the Argyles Nursing Home in Newbury, and had been blind for 20 years. A countrywoman all her life, her story is not just of the privy, but how it fitted into country life nearly a century ago.

'My mother worked as a midwife – a "handywoman" as they were called in those days. She used to charge the women a shilling. When the baby was 10 days old, she would show the mother how to get a small basin and sit the baby on it every time she changed the nappy. After about two weeks, the child would get used to the idea of the toilet. When they got too big for the basin, the mother would use a little pot.

'Our family were farm labourers and we lived in a very small tumbledown cottage. Outside was a very big shed, and everything was kept in there. It was also the loo, which we called the closet. There was always a padlock and chain on the door. It was kept locked all the time because it was in a lonely place on the Berkshire Downs. In those days, there were a lot of what we called travelling people, and every week there would be two or three Romany caravans go by. I was brought up never to be afraid of gypsies. There were two cottages there, and the other one was inhabited by a very old lady who never unlocked her door. Sometimes the gypsies would knock at the door and ask for water, or to enquire if we had any rags and bones for sale. Mother would never turn them away. If there were children, she would always find them a cake or a sweet, and there was never any trouble.

'My father earned 10 shillings a week, and he used to put half

Now sadly derelict, this privy once served the remote farmhouse at Clapton, on the Sutton Estate between Hungerford and Newbury. Surrounded by vigorous vegetation, the old building became a temporary home for a fox, who left his chicken bones behind in a rather untidy pile.

a golden sovereign on the table at 5 pm every Saturday. That was his whole week's wages. In 1911 he got a rise and brought home an extra shilling. That was for working from seven in the morning until five at night, six days a week.

'At the back of the house, there was an enormous horse chestnut tree. When we wanted to make water, we used to have to go behind the tree and "squat up or cock up", depending on what you were born with. The whole family did it – mother and all. I had brothers, but they were older than me.

'The shed with the closet was where dad kept all his tools and a work bench, with logs and bavins and firewood stacked up in there. At the far end was what looked like two boxes. There was a large one, and in the corner a smaller one. Both had a hole cut in the top and a wooden lid with a knob on it, to lift it up by. When I was small I used the little one, and when I got bigger, I used the big one.

'Under the boxes was a very deep pit. To us children, it looked enormous, and it had to be emptied once a year. It was dug out from behind the shed, and there was a big, oval shaped, galvanised metal container with two pivots on either side which swung in a frame on wheels. It would be filled up and wheeled across the road to the field just before the farmer was ready to plough it, so it was dug down into the soil. If it was dry and windy weather, the bits of paper used to blow about all over the place.

'Our prim and proper aunties used to call it "the little house". I didn't like the place at all, I was always afraid I was going to fall in. But mother made me go, and smacked me if I wouldn't. She had an old copper in there, where she used to do the washing. If she smacked you when her hands were wet, it hurt even more.

'After a while, we moved house. There was a cottage going in the village which was much nearer to dad's work. It was in a row of five old cottages which had been condemned. The end one was knocked down, but the middle one wasn't too bad, and the owner repaired it and we moved in. The cottages were in a square next door to the village churchyard. The privies had all gone except for one, right down at the bottom of the garden. It was all overgrown with elder and ivy, and the door was broken in pieces. There was rubbish piled high in there. It was built of weatherboard, and dad cleared it out and smartened it up. The ivy had grown over the roof and in between the weatherboards, some of which were rotten, but the rain did not come in because of the ivy. Dad made a new seat and put it in there with a new bucket. When it was full, he would lift it out and empty it in the garden. It was very lonely down there, with all the tombstones in the churchyard, a long way from the house.

'When it was bedtime, we always wanted to go to the closet, like kids do, just to put off going to bed. The door didn't reach the ground and the mice could get underneath. There were lots of them, and we had five cats in our family. The wind and snow used to blow in under the door. There were always a couple of old coats hanging on the back of the kitchen door, and if it was raining, we used to put one over our head to go to the bottom of the garden. One of my brothers used to have to come with me, although they didn't like to.

'On the other side of the church was the village stores, and they always had loads of wooden boxes that the sides of bacon were delivered in. They were thick, salty boxes. Dad broke them up to make a pigsty next to the privy, everyone kept pigs in those days. There were cube sugar boxes, out of which we used to make rabbit hutches. Dad got a Sunlight soap box and cut a hole in it and made a new seat for me, because I was not big enough for the main hole. There was a little container underneath.

'The laurel and ivy formed a sort of enclosure next to the loo, and we would go in there to make water. We would get into terrible trouble if we peed in the buckets, because that filled them up quickly. There were six in our family, and people often came to visit us.

'Sometimes we were not alone in the loo. There were lots of rats and vermin about in those days, and there were enormous spiders. They would weave the most beautiful webs overnight. They were all so different. Some would have long legs, some with short legs, some with fat bellies and some with thin. But we were never afraid of spiders. Mother kept a stick in there with some turkey feathers tied on the end. When she went down to the closet, she used to brush round the roof to get rid of all the spiders' webs, even though we pleaded with her to leave them. When my prim and proper aunts came over from the next village, they were disgusted with our toilet, but they were much better off than we were. We used to pluck turkeys by hand every Christmas, we all had to muck in. Mother always kept the tail feathers, and made all sorts of things out of them.

'We used to make a noise before we went into the toilet, in case there was a rat in there. The rat would hear the noise and scamper off. Sometimes my father would set a gin trap, and sometimes he would even put it in the bucket, because that's where the rats would go. He would always check the trap before he went to bed at night, in case there was a rat caught in it. If a rat was caught by the leg, it would be in a lot of pain. He did not approve of cruelty. There were a lot of hedgehogs too in the churchyard. I don't know what hedgehogs eat, but the churchyard was infested with enormous slugs. There were great big yellow ones, white ones, black ones and brown ones. On Saturdays, I used to have to go and put flowers on the grave-stones. Those blessed slugs would be all over the headstones at twilight. It made me creep – I hated them.

'The bucket had to be emptied quite often. Dad was a hard

working and enterprising man. He would dig a trench across the gardens and tip the bucket into it, then cover it up with earth. The garden was about half an acre or more, and he would use a different part of it every year, working in rotation. If the bucket had to be emptied and dad wasn't there, one of the boys would have to do it. But they would get into trouble if they didn't dig it deep enough.

'When it came to planting time, we would plant kale, cauliflowers, cabbage, lots of spinach, and Brussels sprouts. They were enormous, like miniature cabbages. Some old toff who came to the village in 1908 started a flower show, and there was a lot of competition to see who could grow the best veg. Believe me, they were far better vegetables than we get today. There is nothing like human manure for gardens.

'But we couldn't use that part of the garden for root vegetables until the following year. Then we would plant carrots, parsnips, turnips and radishes – and we always had a row of mustard and cress. We used to cut some on Saturday afternoons for tea.

'We lived there for a long time. My mother died there in 1950. She would not move, and my dad had died there and was buried next to the church. He died in 1918.

'It was all pulled down after she died and the place was sold. There is a nice big house there now.

'Father got some weatherboard and built a new toilet nearer the house, so we would not have to go all the way to the bottom of the garden. He built it big enough to have the little box for me, and there was a box of ashes. These had to be sifted and the fine ash sprinkled down the hole to keep the flies away. The big bits of ash went back on the fire. We children always put too much ash down the hole and filled the bucket up, so were in trouble again.

'We used to tear up squares of newspaper, poke a skewer through one corner and thread a string through to hang it up with. We had the *Christian Herald* regularly, my brother used to read it. All sorts of books would be used when there was no paper left on the string. Some of them were not at all suitable, and were printed on paper that was stiff and shiny. Dad built a little enclosure at the side for us to make water and save filling up the bucket. When father died in 1918, there was no more wages coming in, and I had to go out to domestic service in a big house, gentry it was. I started as a kitchen maid, and in one of the rooms of the house was an old lady. She was very old and a semi-invalid.

'In one corner of the room was a thing like a queer looking armchair. It looked like a box with arms and a back, and a hole in the middle of the seat. One of my jobs was looking after the kitchen range, and the ashes had to be taken out to the gardener. I would have to take a little box of fine ashes up to this room. I hated the job, but I wish now I had taken more notice. There was a handle on one side of the box. When you pulled the handle up, it spread some of the ash into the hole. Where it went after that I have no idea. I just had to tip the ash in. I have never seen anything like it since. I've seen them where you pull the handle and the water flushes, but nothing like this.

'When I was a small child, mother and us children used to have to walk about a mile to the chapel, down very lonely country lanes. At the top of the lane, there was a gateway with some hayricks. When we got there, mother and my auntie would say to us girls to go and squat up behind the rick, and make sure we didn't step in any old iron. I have done that many a time behind that rick. Now, old iron was where the men went and done a major job and wiped their selves with a dock leaf. There was always plenty of dock leaves there, and the old women used to go a-dockin', collecting them in their aprons, when the corn was just coming up. A lot of the docks just seeded there by the hedge. The leaves were the best thing for wiping your behind with.

Miss Taylor's chapel at Leckhampstead Thicket. The sign over the door says 'Primitive Methodist'; enough said.

'But there were a lot of thistles and nettles as well, when you got into the herbiage that had not been cut. We never knew whether we were going to get a sting or a prick or whatever. It was most uncomfortable if we had to go to chapel after we had sat on a stinging nettle or a thistle.

'Often, we did step in a piece of old iron, and mother would wipe it off our shoes with a handful of grass. The problem came when we had to climb over the gate. If someone had stepped in the old iron and not wiped their shoes, it got all over the gate, and the next person over it would get their clothes plastered with this muck. It happened to me many a time, and we would get into terrible trouble, with smacked legs and lots of tears.

'When we got over the gate to go behind the hedge, it was nothing to see someone coming out of a gap in the hedge. You used to have to walk everywhere in those days, if you didn't have a bicycle or a pony and trap.

'At the chapel we went to, they used to start the service at about 6 pm, us kids used to get very fidgety. We didn't mind the singing, but the preacher always went on and on. At the end, there was always some old man who would say that we would have a prayer meeting, and so we'd be there another hour. Oh, it was boring. The parson would go, because he would have to walk to Compton. After a while, we would want to go to the toilet. If it was dark when we came out of chapel, we would just go by the side of the road.

'When the men on the farms went out with horses and wagons, to take corn to Doltons the corn merchants, or to Newbury station, they were allowed to stop and urinate by the nearside wheel of the wagon, because they were not allowed to leave the horses.

'I hope you have enjoyed my story. I realise it's not the sort of thing to read at teatime.'

[5]

An Unenviable Task

Spare a thought, if you have not already, for those whose lot it was to empty the bucket or the pit. Not everyone had the compensation of an enriched and flourishing garden to encourage them.

Mr H. J. Edwards of Hungerford has memories of the outside privy that go back to the 1920s.

'The toilet consisted of a rough wooden shed at the far end of the garden. In the shed were two seats at different heights, one for children and one for the adults. Under the seat was an earth pit, which had to be emptied out with a scoop on the end of a long handle.

'Later on in life, when I got married, we had the bucket type toilet in the garden. This had to be emptied weekly, and my wife had to scrub and disinfect it.

'There was no toilet paper around like there is now, and we had to cut newspaper into squares. At night, we had to carry a candle in a jam jar with string for a handle. Later on we used to use a paraffin hurricane lamp.

'Some time after that, two men started coming round with a motor tanker every week to empty the buckets and disinfect them. They used to charge one shilling for this service, and it was always done at night. We used to leave the shilling in a secret place in the toilet, so only they would know where to find it.'

Mr T. C. Sumner of Sunninghill recalls his childhood in the east of the county. 'I was born in 1916, and two years later my father took over as caretaker of Sunningdale Church of England School, living on the premises. This was a fairly large school,

A traditional emptying scoop — the type once used by local councils on their weekly honeycart emptying sessions.

consisting of the main building and a separate infants school.

'The toilets were three rows of brick buildings in the playground, as far away from the school as possible. All had buckets which my father had to empty every evening. They were emptied onto a spare bit of ground just outside the school boundary and covered over with a bit of soil. There was one block of toilets for the boys and one for the girls, and a smaller one for the infants aged five to seven. The first toilet in each block was for the teachers.

'There were no toilet rolls, only newspaper. To use the toilet meant a walk of at least 50 yards in all weathers. There were two sinks in the main school and one in the infants, each with a cold tap – no hot water in those days, and one roller towel to each sink, which had to last a week. The main sewer was laid through the village in the mid-1920s, but very few houses were connected at that time.

'I have vivid memories of the night cart coming round. This was a horse-drawn tank on wheels, which went round after dark.

'The school was eventually connected up to the main sewer, and although they had flush toilets, they still remained in the same position in the playground until after the last war.'

WHERE DID THE RAT BITE YOU?

Mr Ronald Boyle of Windsor is an expert on sanitary matters, having spent a lifetime in the business. 'Having spent almost all my working life in the sewers, I have a number of items to contribute,' he told me.

'A lady complained that a rat had bitten her whilst she was in occupation. I had to warn the rather rough diamond of a sewer foreman not to say "Madam, I have come to see where the rat bit you". This was at a row of houses where the drain passed under all the outside toilets and they dropped straight down into it with no water trap. Many of these toilets had no flushing tank, and people had to flush them out with a bucket of water.

'That type of arrangement was common in outdoor toilets in old schools and, I am told, in wartime army camps. My father used to tell the story of the school where the pipe passed under adjacent boys' and girls' toilets.

'One of the boys got a long ostrich feather to tickle the girl in the next cubicle. Unfortunately for him, it was a lady teacher.

'Wartime stories include ones of failed flushing systems being replaced by a constantly running hosepipe. Soldiers would make little boats out of newspaper and set fire to them, then float them down the water channel which ran under the row of holes in the latrine. Unsuspecting squaddies would howl with agony as the burning paper floated under their most tender regions. But the perpetrators always beat a hasty retreat. Retribution would have been terrible.'

Mr Boyle remembers that when the 'bucket and chuck it' era started to come to an end and main drains took the strain, cold weather would cause enormous problems, with pipes and tanks freezing up.

'The old outside privies were gradually converted to the flush, but would often freeze up in winter, no matter how much lagging their owners wrapped round the pipes.

'One chap whose privy was next to the kitchen had a clever idea. He installed the water flush tank high on the wall inside the kitchen, which was always warm, knocked a hole in the wall and connected the down pipe to the lavatory pan on the other side. An ingenious linking system made it possible for the chain to be pulled from the privy, but it was a little unnerving for visitors who were in the kitchen and unaware of this peculiar item of plumbing. Even more unnerving was when the resident of the house decided to play a prank on unsuspecting users of the toilet, by pulling the chain in the kitchen while they were sitting on the loo.'

[6]

PRIVIES WITH A PAST

MURDER MOST FOUL

An undistinguished looking privy at Walkers Lane in Lambourn has been witness to more than one violent death over the years.

It stands in a garden in front of a row of cottages, one of which was the home of a jockey called Derrick Cheshire, who lived there in 1930. Cheshire had an argument with his neighbours, the Giddings family, and two of the sons, Ted and Fred Giddings, attacked Cheshire at his own front door. Cheshire took out his knife and slashed Ted across the arm, then embedded it up to the hilt in Fred's neck. He died later in Newbury Hospital.

Cheshire was charged with murder but pleaded self defence. He was found not guilty after just six minutes by the jury at Birmingham Assizes, and witnesses for both prosecution and defence all went home together on the bus. Ted Giddings later accidentally shot himself while out hunting rabbits. He was killed instantly.

In 1936, Thomas and Lizzie Townsend moved into the cottage. He blasted her to death with a shotgun after an argument about money. He was found guilty, with the jury making a recommendation for mercy. The judge sentenced him to hang, but this was commuted to life imprisonment, only days before he was due to be executed. He spent the last years of his life in Broadmoor.

In recent years, the cottage has been the home of racing columnist Charlie Morlock, a person of impeccable character, so he tells me.

A privy with memories – Walkers Lane, Lambourn.

Many people will still remember the underground public conveniences in Reading's Butter Market. In the austere times immediately after the Second World War, with queues still common and coupons needed for many everyday items, the council simply stuck up signs saying 'Men' and 'Women'. Later this was changed to 'Gentlemen' and 'Ladies'. Perhaps the Corporation thought this might attract a better class of customer.

Sadly, these facilities are no longer available to the people of the town. Even the little car park, with its cantankerous parking attendant and the small wooden hut where he brewed up his tea, is long gone, as are the public toilets at St Mary's Butts and Caversham Bridge.

This photograph of the old public conveniences built underground in Reading's Butter Market was taken soon after the Second World War.

A perfectly preserved pair of privies are the pride and joy of Mrs
Cindy Cooper and are at the bottom of her garden at Woolton
Hill, near Newbury. Mrs Cooper, a New Yorker by birth, and
her husband bought their 15th-century cottage in a derelict
state several years ago and have spent countless hours restoring
it to its original condition. She even took a college course to learn
the ancient art of wattle and daub, and how to work with natural
lime. The first thing on the agenda for restoration was the privy,
because the house had no bathroom, and Mr and Mrs Cooper
had to put up with the outside loo until plumbing was installed.
The house – and the privy – are now in tip top condition.

An excellent two-holer still exists – although almost completely
hidden under the foliage that has grown up around it – at
Burchett's Green, near Maidenhead. It is in the back garden of
a former alehouse, the Greyhound, which closed down in the
1970s, when the elderly landlady, Mrs Ivy Pratt, decided to
retire. She carried on living in the house, and was using the
privy up until 1987, when her daughter persuaded her to have
an inside flush loo installed.

Mrs Pratt was still able to enjoy a drink in the village's other
pub, directly across the road, but after a glass or two she sometimes got disorientated and had to be shown the way home.

Her old privy is built over a deep hole, which flushes away to a
pit a few feet away at the bottom of the garden. It had to be emptied once a year and was covered with sheets of corrugated iron.

Her next door neighbour remembers making himself scarce at
emptying time, although Ivy would come round to try and
cadge more corrugated iron sheeting, which rapidly went rusty
and fell to bits because of the pungent nature of the contents of
the pit.

When he moved in 20 years ago, his privy was a 'bucket and

Mrs Cooper's wonderfully restored privies at Woolton Hill.

Deep in the undergrowth at Burchett's Green.

chuck it' in the back yard, and is now used as a coal shed.

The Greyhound is now the home of Paul and Jackie Loudon, who moved in with a long list of jobs to do on the house. The privy is nowhere near the top of the list, but they do intend to restore it to its former glory.

A Rolls Royce of privies stands in the garden of a beamed cottage at Hill Green, near Leckhampsted, which was for a short time the home of former Newbury MP Mrs Judith Chaplin, who died in 1994.

We do not know if Mrs Chaplin ever used the privy, even though it is such a fine example with real style. The seat has

The parent and child two-holer in the back garden of the former Greyhound.

The splendid wooden thatched privy at Hill Green.

been very carefully made, with the lid being cut out from the middle to form the hole. The joiner who made it then put a small handle on the lid so that it could be taken off and put back on by dainty little hands.

The cottage is now the home of Mr and Mrs Ian Hocking, who are rightly proud of their privy – but will stick with the indoor plumbing for the time being.

The Thames Valley Police training school at Sulhamstead House, south-west of Reading, was originally the home of the Thoyts family, who had a rare example of a Victorian flush loo installed; see picture on next page.

The police moved into the house and 60 acres of grounds in 1952. It is also the home of the Force museum, which contains a number of items from the Great Train Robbery of 1963, including the Monopoly board the gang used to while away the time – playing with real cash.

The police are very proud of the old loo, which is still in good working order and has been graced with a plethora of police posteriors.

LISTED LOO

The old privy at the Manor House in East Ilsley is a listed building, Grade 2. This is because it is built into the structure of the old walled garden (see picture on page 66). The beautiful house is probably 17th century, but the loo is not quite as old. It has not been used for many years – if you can afford a house like this, you can afford plumbing. Even so, the rhubarb behind the privy is doing very well.

The police at Sulhamstead House are very proud of their old loo.

Architect David Smith acquired his house at Eling in 1981. It had been a derelict row of three farm cottages, owned by the Eling Estate. He bought them at auction and set about making them into a habitable dwelling.

The sanitary arrangements were primitive. One old privy outside the back door was falling down, so he demolished it. There was another in the garden, about 30 yards from the house, but it needed new weatherboarding and had holes in the roof; see pictures on pages 68 and 69.

Mr Smith patched it up and used the privy for almost a year, all through the winter of 1981/82. He remembers trudging through the snow with a torch: 'It was very bracing, to say the least'.

The new plumbing was installed, and the privy was redundant. But Mr Smith will not demolish it. In fact he intends to replace the worm-eaten woodwork inside it. 'It is well worth preserving,' he said.

There's a delightful little dunny nestling under a huge yew tree at Ashford Hill, near Newbury, that was still in regular use as late as 1997; see picture on page 69. It was in the garden of a tiny two-room cottage owned by the Hutchins family. Mr Norman Hutchins lived there from 1952 until his death. When he first moved in, a solemn-faced inspector from the local council declared the early 18th-century cottage 'unsuitable for habitation'. There was no sanitation, running water or electricity and Mr Hutchins used candles, the privy, and drew water from a 20-foot well in the yard. No problem with freezing pipes in winter.

Local builder Brian Watts bought the property after Mr Hutchins died and he built a very nice house in the grounds. He had to go on a course to learn how to use wattle and daub and limewash to restore the cottage, now a listed building, to its original condition.

The listed loo at the Manor House, East Ilsey – see page 63.

Mrs Ellen Hurlock left Newport in Monmouthshire in the 1940s and settled down with her husband in a Victorian terrace house at Eton Wick. Now a widow, she still has a little privy in the back yard, although it has been converted to flush; see picture on page 70.

That brings problems, because the pipes freeze up in winter, despite the insulation.

She told me 'When it gets really cold, I go and stay with my son in Bracknell. He's got central heating.'

The 30 yard dash at Eling – very bracing in the snow; see page 65.

Inside Mr Smith's privy at Eling; see page 65.

A tranquil scene at Ashford Hill; see page 65.

Mrs Hurlock's privy at Eton Wick; see page 67.

[7]

RECYCLED PRIVIES

What useful little buildings they are . . .

KINTBURY

Any drinking man over the age of 40 will remember the bad old days of the outside loo at the village pub – some of them didn't even have a roof. Not much fun on a cold winter's night when it was pouring with rain.

At least the one at the Blue Ball at Kintbury had a tin roof, which made a racket like a machine gun when it was raining hard. It is now redundant and used for storage, having been replaced by an inside loo.

Old pub loos rarely had electric light, and few publicans would leave a hurricane lamp to illuminate the most essential part of the evening's business. They worked on the theory that either you were a regular and could find your way in the dark – or you were desperate and could find your way in the dark.

The urinal stall was usually just a shallow channel along the base of one wall, with a drain at one end. Up to waist height, the wall would be covered with a sort of filthy black tar, often peeling off in large lumps. Worst of all was the smell, which was always appalling and lingered long in the nostrils. And how many times have you seen scribbled on the wall 'Please do not chuck your dog ends in the urinal. It makes them soggy and difficult to light'!

This charming little house stands in a garden at Woolton Hill. It is now a store for garden tools.

The former loo at the Blue Ball, Kintbury.

HUNGERFORD

There's a marvellous line of redundant privies to be seen in Hungerford – they were formerly used by the people who lived in the cottages at The Croft. These invaluable adjuncts to modern-day living now store everything from lawnmowers to coal.

The art of conversation is probably dying because no one builds rows of privies like this any more. All cooped up together, first thing in the morning, it would have been impossible to ignore your neighbours – but exactly what you would talk to them about under such circumstances is best left to the imagination.

The row of former privies at The Croft, Hungerford.

UFTON NERVET

At Ufton Court, a spectacular Elizabethan mansion at Ufton Nervet, to the south-west of Reading, there are two modest little loos under the stone steps that lead down from the terrace to the lawn. They were built into the steps for the convenience of people playing bowls or croquet on the green. Now long disused, they are stores for hockey sticks and old footballs.

Ufton Court is part of the Englefield Estate, owned by the Benyon family. The estate has a large number of farms, houses and cottages. Richard Benyon told me that a modernisation programme was implemented in the 1960s, when all the traditional old privies were replaced by flush loos. 'Some of the older tenants objected most strongly to having the loo moved inside,' said Mr Benyon. 'They thought it was most unhygienic.'

74

Below the terrace at Ufton Court.

The former Edwardian public conveniences from the tram station at Caversham Bridge, now at the Chilterns Open Air Museum.

An old Englefield tenant told me, 'I dunno what the world's coming to. When I was a lad, we ate our meals in the house and went down the garden to the privy. Now we have a barbecue on the patio and come in the house for a shit.'

STILL GOING STRONG!

The wonderful Edwardian public convenience erected by Reading Corporation in 1906 at the tram terminus at Caversham Bridge is sorely missed in the town. For reasons best known to themselves, the council decided to demolish it in 1985, and it was dismantled piece by piece by volunteers and moved to the Chilterns Open Air Museum at Chalfont St Giles, where it has

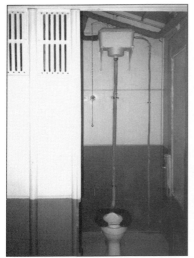

High cistern – good flush.

De luxe urinal stalls made by Twyfords of Hanley in Staffs.

Ornate loo roll holder.

'No towels are to be issued except in a sealed wrapper . . .'

This recycled privy at a house on the Yattendon Estate is now a coal shed –
but it still has the cucumber frame alongside.

been recycled as what it was in the first place – a public toilet.
Painted in its original Brunswick Green, it is in full working con-
dition and is used by museum visitors. It won the 'Loo of the
Year Award' for London and the Home Counties in 1992.

The building is made entirely of cast iron panels from the
Saracen Foundry in Glasgow. The Corporation paid £301 for
the structure, and £750 for building and plumbing – including
gas lighting. It was open daily from 6 am to midnight, with an
attendant at the ready with clean towels and a hot tip for the
races.

This privy on the Yattendon Estate was converted very carefully and now houses a freezer.

A really novel form of recycling. This privy at Yattendon is now a goal post for children's basketball.

[8]

WARTIME MEMORIES

THE STENCH OF WAR

During the war, Berkshire had to find space for thousands of American soldiers in the run up to D-Day. Feeding them was not a problem, rations came from the USA in copious amounts. It was getting rid of the end product that was difficult. Uncle Sam didn't send any tankers over to take it all back, so it had to be disposed of locally. Didn't the rhubarb grow well.

The 501st Parachute Infantry Regiment were camped in tents in the fields between Enborne and Hamstead Marshall. Over 1,000 men had to share a tent with a row of buckets under benches with holes in them. Former sergeant Clyde Grube remembers, 'My tent was next to the "honey bucket tent". That was OK for when you needed to use it, but when the "honey cart men" came with a tank on wheels to empty the buckets, you really had to hold your nose. No one ever knew where they took it all, no one really cared.'

Paul Quaiver was an engineer from Chicago, stationed in the grounds of Basildon House. 'When we arrived, the first thing we wanted was the latrine,' he said. 'We just followed our noses. It was a very sombre place, with a very strong smell of disinfectant. I was a short GI, and mounting those seats was a bit of a chore. Most of us feared we might fall in, but we got used to it. A small truck with a tank on it used to drive up to collect our offerings. The collectors would tip all the buckets down a hole in the top of the tank. When they'd finished, they would drive down to the mess, and the mess sergeant would make them a sandwich. They would drive off, munching their reward.'

Corporal Paul Quaiver outside the 'honey bucket hut' at Basildon House.

Some of the old GIs tell the story of a soldier who borrowed an officer's Jeep to go out with a local girl. On the way home it was dark, and no lights were permitted because of the blackout. The soldier knew the road, and was showing off to his girlfriend by driving far too fast. What he didn't know was that the honey cart was on its way home at the end of the day, driving slowly and with no lights.

The Jeep hit it in the rear at speed. The contents surged forward and drenched the driver and his mate, then surged back and poured gallons and gallons of filth all over the Jeep, the soldier and the girl. They were covered in it. Needless to say, that was the end of a budding romance, and the GI got a roasting from his commanding officer. He also had to clean the Jeep, which next morning was covered in a thick crust of foul smelling sewage. He walked everywhere after that.

Peter Ustinov's memories of National Service are included in his autobiography, where he tells of military efficiency imposed on the latrines.

Two soldiers were detailed to tidy up the outside loos at a barracks. One was sweeping up stray bits of toilet paper while the other held a bin to collect them. A sudden gust of wind caught a well-soiled piece and blew it across the parade ground, high in the air, and through the colonel's open window. One of the soldiers hurried in pursuit of the errant paper. He returned a while later, hands in pockets and with a disconsolate expression.

'Didn't you get it?' asked the other.

'No,' he replied. 'The colonel had already signed it.'

Shrewsbury Terrace is a row of a dozen houses built by the Great

The all-purpose sheds at Shrewsbury Terrace, Newbury.

Western Railway in about 1850 for rail workers at Newbury station. The houses were tiny, and right outside the front door was a bucket privy, store shed and wash house.

Mr Doug Fish and his wife Grace scraped together the £50 deposit they needed to buy one of them in 1947, after he was discharged from the army. The couple still live there, but Mr Fish has installed more modern facilities inside the house.

He clearly remembers using the outside 'bucket and chuck it' loo for quite some time after he moved in, but Mr Fish had got used to much worse sanitary arrangements – he had spent nearly three years as a prisoner of war in Germany and Poland, where he was kept in a camp next door to the notorious Auschwitz.

In his famous book *If this is a Man*, Italian author Primo Levi recalls the appalling sanitary conditions at Auschwitz, and how the Jewish prisoners would scramble to get the job of 'Scheiss-minister', or toilet cleaner, because it was less arduous or disgusting than some of the other tasks they were forced to do. Levi had fought with the partisans in Italy. He was captured by the Germans and ended up as a 'Haeftling', or Jewish prisoner, in the camp called Monowitz Buna, next door to Auschwitz.

'The latrine is an oasis of peace,' he wrote. 'It is a provisional latrine which the Germans have not yet provided with the customary wooden partitions to separate the various divisions: "Only for English prisoners", "Only for Poles", "Only for Ukrainian women", and so on, with, a little apart, "Only for Haeftlinge". Inside, shoulder by shoulder, sit four hollow faced Haeftlinge; a bearded old Russian worker, a Polish boy and an English PoW, his face splendidly shaven and rosy, and his khaki uniform neat, ironed and clean.'

Mr Levi recalled that they used to call the bucket under the seat 'Jules', and emptying it was referred to as 'taking Jules by the ears'.

Lt Col Frank Hynes, who lives at Brimpton, recalls being captured by the Germans in Italy during the last war.

As a young paratrooper, Col Hynes was involved in a daring raid on a German position. He was captured, escaped, was recaptured, escaped again and finally made it home to England to rejoin his unit, the 1st Airborne Division. His first day of captivity was with a group of other PoWs in a barn in Southern Italy, with no facilities whatever. By the end of the day, the need for relief was becoming urgent for many of them.

They called to the German guard and asked him to let them out, which he did, keeping a firm grip on his sub-machine gun.

Italy had changed sides in the war the previous day, and the morale of the German troops was considerably affected.

The captured soldiers asked where they could go and defecate. The guard told them, 'Listen, Englishmen. This is Italy. As far as I am concerned, you can shit wherever you like.'

[9]

On The Throne

Windsor is undoubtedly England's finest castle, and gives Berkshire its 'Royal' title. Sadly, it is the only one left in the county worthy of note, all the others having been badly knocked about by Roundheads and Cavaliers in the Civil War of the 1640s.

If you are Royalty and live six floors up in a huge, impressive castle and need to expedite the Royal We, it is a bit of a pain to have to walk down an endless spiral staircase, trip over the cat, cross the courtyard, have the guards raise the portcullis and let down the drawbridge to get to the outside privy every time you need the toilet – especially at night.

Castle builders soon cottoned on that their customers wanted – quite literally – a convenience, and came up with the 'garderobe'. This is Norman French for a wardrobe, or cloakroom, which is an odd word in this context because the Latin word cloaca means a sewer.

The garderobe, as we have seen in chapter 1, was a little cupboard built into the castle wall, with a pipe running through to deposit the privy product in the moat, which rapidly turned from being a defensive measure into something very offensive. Chucking that stuff down on your enemies' heads was twice as effective as boiling oil. The garderobe was usually quite high up to prevent invaders sneaking in. There is nothing more disconcerting, whether you are royalty or not, than to be sitting peacefully in the garderobe when some bugger starts prodding you with a spear.

The tiny closets were used to store clothes as well as housing the loo, which, along with the fact they never bathed, is probably why everyone smelled so dreadful. In summer the pong was

The garderobes looked a bit like this. In this case, the top of the tower is designed so that rainwater runs off easily – and the sentry doesn't have to leave his post.

disgusting, and in winter they were very, very cold.

Edward III ordered that privies be built at Windsor, for his Knights of the Garter, an order which he founded in 1348. New accommodation for the 25 'poor knights' was built into the castle wall, including garderobes. Most surprisingly, he paid for the work out of his own pocket — the privy purse. How much he spent is not clear, as workmen and suppliers were paid piecemeal as soon as a job was finished. It seems this was the only way they would agree to do the job, as the working men did not trust the nobility to pay up on time — if at all.

The architectural records show that these garderobes were later abandoned. The castle does not have a moat and is not on the river bank. The contents of the garderobes, therefore, landed on the ground at the foot of the castle walls and stayed there. Guards on night time patrol had to be extremely careful. If you trod that stuff into the guardhouse, the sergeant got very cross indeed. Today, there is not a garderobe left — and today's occupiers of this ancient accommodation, the Military Knights of Windsor, all have modern facilities, I am glad to say.

Windsor town suffered problems with sewage disposal for centuries. In 1844 there were 53 overflowing cesspits at the castle. The stuff was running down the streets, and Prince Albert, Queen Victoria's husband, insisted that proper drains be installed, for the sake of everyone's health. The poor chap died of typhoid anyway in 1861 at the age of 42.

But the new drains often got blocked, and the forerunners of Dyno-Rod set up in business with a variety of solutions. Probably the most bizarre was an explosive device called 'The Pain's Drain Rocket'. The company, which later confined itself to making much prettier fireworks, reckoned the rocket was a sure fire way of shifting the blockage.

They probably also shifted quite a lot of people off the toilet, and very quickly too. I for one would not want to be on the loo while Mr Pain was playing with such dangerous toys. He might have lived up to his name a bit too closely for my liking.

To go back a few years, George II died while literally on the throne. He was seated in his closet one day in 1760, when his valet heard a noise 'louder than the Royal Wind'. He rushed in to find the King flat on his face on the floor of the privy, stone dead.

[1 0]

The Ploughman's Hat

A farmer at Upper Basildon bought one of the first tractors to be seen in Berkshire. It was delivered to the farm, and the ploughman was summoned for instructions on how to work it.

The farmer told him what he could remember of the salesman's instructions. It was an early model which started up on petrol, and then switched to agricultural fuel oil. The pedal on the right made it go faster, and the one on the left made it stop.

The other thing the farmer remembered from the salesman's spiel was 'Grease everything that moves – every day'. The farmer laid particular emphasis on this, and pointed to a large tub of grease in the corner of the stable yard. The ploughman did as he was bid, picking up dollops of grease by the handful and liberally applying it to every moving part.

One morning, he could not find a rag to wipe his hands on, so he wiped them on his hat. It was a warm day, and after a while, the hat started to smell rather strongly. When he went home to his wife, she complained of the smell and insisted on washing the hat.

To no effect. The hat hung on the washing line, just as greasy and smelly as before. She told him he would have to find something to get the grease out. The next evening, he returned home with a gallon of petrol, which someone had assured him would get rid of the grease. He told his wife to be very careful with it, because it was 'really powerful stuff'.

Next morning she set to work with the petrol, finishing off with a bucket of soapsuds. The hat was as good as new, but she had more than half the petrol left. Remembering her husband's warning, she decided she had better dispose of it safely. The obvious place was down the privy, an old pit-type earth closet.

The ploughman came home for lunch, and afterwards wandered down the garden to the privy. Comfortably seated, he took out his pipe, carefully lit it, and dropped the match down the hole.

The explosion blew the roof off the rickety privy, and the ploughman shot out of the door, trousers round his ankles, angry and bewildered. He was not seriously hurt – but he spent the next few days driving the tractor standing up.

[1 1]

GRAFFITI

This little book has concentrated mainly on the country privy, the 'little house' at the end of a garden path, a solitary destination – or shared with one other – or two – or three at the most.

I couldn't end, however, without remarking on a more public activity – writing on walls. And Berkshire's graffitists are second to none:

The painter's work is all in vain, the piss-house poet strikes again. Kilroy was here. Wot? No paper?

Butter Market, Reading

In days of old when knights were bold,
And lavatories weren't invented,
They did their load in the middle of the road,
And went away contented.

Caversham

Stand closer, it may be shorter than you think.

Pangbourne

(*High up on wall*) While you are reading this, you are piddling on your shoes.

St Mary's Butts, Reading

It's no good looking up here for a joke – you've got one in your hand.

Reading pub

The future of Britain is in your hands.

Reading Town Hall

Here sits me, broken hearted. Paid a penny and only farted.

Butter Market, Reading

O O A Q I C I 8 2 Q B 4 I P

Maidenhead

I do not like this place at all,
The seat is too high and the hole is too small.
Your poem prompts this sharp retort –
Your bum is too big and your legs are too short.

Corn Exchange, Newbury

All this beer will be the urination of me.

Pub at Hungerford

Any complaints must be made to the new Urinary Authority.

Gents at Theale

A Privy By Any Other Name

A certain place
Any old iron
Bathroom
Bog
Bog house
Closet
Comfort station
Crap house
Dumping ground
Dunnekin
Dunny
Dyke
Evacuation station
Garden loo
Garderobe
Gents
Going for a Jimmy Riddle
   (or – for the toffs – Going
   for a James Rideaux)
Going for a piddle
Going for a pony and trap
Going for a strain
Going for a Tom Tit
Going to let the drain take the
   strain
Going to pick daisies
Going to powder my nose

Going to see a man about
   a dog
Going to wash one's hands
Heads (in the Navy)
Holy of holies
Houses of Parliament
Jakes
John
Karzy
Ladies
Latrines
Lav
Lavatory
Little boys' room
Little girls' room
Little house
Loo
My aunt's
Out the back
Pisshouse
Place of easement
Point Percy at the porcelain
Poo house
Proverbial
Reading Room (the name
   of a former Editor's
   house)

Round the back
Shit hole
Shit house
Slash hole
Slash house
Spend a penny
The men's room (on US
    air bases)
The necessary
The offices
The um, thingy

The wossname
Throne room
Thunder box
Toilet
Urinal
Waterloo
Wee house
Widdlehouse
Wotchermecallit
Yer tiz
You know where